HIGH SPIRITS

First published in the UK in 2023 by
Clearview Books
99 Priory Park Road
London NW6 7UX
www.clearviewbooks.com

© Text Sam de Terán
© Illustrations Isabelle Feliu

ISBN 978-1908337-719

Art Direction: Sam de Terán
Project Management: Catharine Snow
Design: Lucy Gowans
Production: Rosanna Dickinson

A CIP record of this book is available from the British Library.

Printed in Italy.

HIGH SPIRITS
EASY ELEGANT COCKTAILS

SAM DE TERÁN

ILLUSTRATED BY
ISABELLE FELIU

CLEARVIEW BOOKS

TO GOOD TIMES & TO THE FRIENDS
WITH WHOM WE SHARE THEM

My expertise is limited to the seated side of the bar but I know a good cocktail when I drink it & my favourites - the freshest & the cleanest - are all in here. I grew up in Madrid drinking Cuba Libres, an excellent any-hour drink, but only if the ice is cold & the lime is fresh. As with any cocktail, the citrus must be fresh - no packaged citrus, whatever it says on the packet, tastes as bright as the one you've just squeezed. The glass should be chilled because a cold cocktail in a warm glass is as disappointing as hot food on a cold plate.

The drink must be cold, the citrus must be fresh & go easy on the syrup.

That's 90% of what you need to know & if you stick to this formula your cocktails will be as clean & bright as citrus & sunshine. They'll be lean too, because the 'sweet' quantities have been adjusted for modern tastes.

To keep things easy & light, I prefer drinks with only one liquor. If the occasional dash of liqueur is added it serves for flavour & to replace the syrup element. If you prefer to take your vodka, rum, gin, tequila & triple sec all at the same time & in the same glass (I'm not joking, that's a Long Island Iced Tea), then you should probably get help, this book isn't for you.

Use these recipes & you won't be doing anything silly like sieving strawberries or mixing sticky batches of syrup. Don't bother to dress your drinks with much more than a twist or wheel of citrus - anything else just gets in the way or stuck in your teeth. Avoid Maraschino cherries at all times, never use a straw after dark, never use the word 'garnish' & always go easy on the sugar.

CONTENTS

FEELING SO STYLISH & WORLDLY
WITH MY COCKTAIL SHAKER ...

WHAT YOU'LL NEED

WHAT YOU'LL NEED: IMPLEMENTS

You'll probably have most of these already, except perhaps a jigger & a cocktail shaker. If you were to make all the cocktails in this book you'd need all these items, but most drinks can be made with just a cold glass, ice & the ingredients.

IF YOU BUY NOTHING ELSE, BUY:

Cocktail Shaker (not glass & with a tight fitting lid).
Jigger (in oz to measure the liquor).

IF YOU CAN, BUY:

Muddler to crush ingredients (but a wooden spoon or rolling pin will do).
Hawthorne Strainer (to strain liquids from the shaker into the glass).
Bar Spoon (a long handled spoon useful for stirring ingredients, measuring syrup & tasting).
Straws (paper)

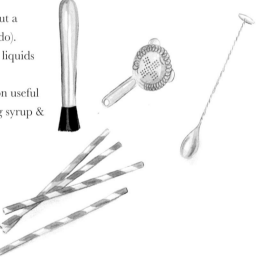

**All these implements & more are available from www.amathusdrinks.com.
Store locations at amathusdrinks.com/amathus-stores**

YOU'LL PROBABLY ALREADY HAVE:

Blender (only for fruity cocktails).
Citrus squeezer (a fork will do).
Ice Trays (large cubes, large balls, small cubes).
Jug (any largish vessel).
Nutmeg grater (any fine grater will do).
Paring Knife (any sharp knife will do).
Teaspoon (or set of measuring spoons.
If using a bar spoon, remember a teaspoon
holds slightly more than a bar spoon).

A NOTE ON TERMINOLOGY

You'll sound like a pro if you bandy these terms about a bit.

BLENDING: as it sounds. I use a stick blender but the pros prefer a proper big blender.

BUILDING: a fine, easy way to make a cocktail is to build it in the glass in which you'll serve it.

EXPRESSING: pressing a section of citrus peel between thumb & forefinger to spritz out the lemon oil - you'll see the oil floating on the surface of the drink & the zing of it really does make a difference.

MUDDLING: crushing something - generally lime, lemon or mint.

RIMMING: rubbing a lime or lemon wedge around the top edge of a glass, then dipping the glass into salt.

STRAINING: sieving ice, fruit or herbs out before pouring.

TOPPING: as you'd imagine, topping up to the rim - generally with soda.

WHAT YOU'LL NEED: GLASSES

In a fix, any old glass will do so long as it's cold but, in a perfect world, you'd have:
HIGHBALL, ROCKS & COUPE GLASSES.

You might think it's fun to have these three too:
MARGARITA, MARTINI & HURRICANE GLASSES.

The coupe glass above easily replaces both a Martini & a Margarita glass.

WHAT YOU'LL NEED: INGREDIENTS

SOME OF SOUR, LESS OF SWEET,
SOME OF STRONG, MORE OF WEAK.

i.e. Citrus + Syrup + Spirits + Ice

THE SOUR: CITRUS

There is NO substitute for freshly squeezed citrus. Get the citrus right
& all will be well. I give measurements in oz & in actual fruit, so, if you
don't have the inclination to measure your citrus juice with a jigger, use
this rule of thumb:

$^1/_2$ a large lime produces roughly $^1/_2$ oz of lime juice.
1 large lime will produce 1oz & so on.

$^1/_2$ a small lemon produces roughly $^1/_2$ oz lemon juice.
1 small lemon produces 1oz & so on.

Most cocktails require the juice of one lemon or one lime, depending on
personal taste & the size & juiciness of the citrus.

THE SWEET: THE SUGAR, SYRUP or NECTAR

Most drinks can be made 'skinny' i.e. without any 'sweet' at all, so
whatever type of 'sweet' you use, go easy, consider it optional, add
sparingly & to taste. The measures of 'sweet' I give are for a neat syrup
because a neat syrup is just quicker & cleaner than messing around with
batches of a sugar & water mix.

It's much easier too, to measure out your neat syrup in a bar spoon if you
have one or a household teaspoon if you don't, rather than using a jigger
for oz quantities.

There are so many good syrup options out there these days; demerara, maple, agave, yacon, coconut blossom syrup etc. I tend to use a light agave or yacon syrup in most drinks, maple syrup in an Old Fashioned & demerara sugar for a Mojito & a Caipirinha. Just use whichever 'sweet' you keep at home, but avoid honey or Erithrytol as their flavour is too strong.

NEAT SYRUP MEASURES: OUNCES TO BARSPOONS

NEAT SYRUP IN OZ	NEAT SYRUP IN BARSPOONS
$1/4$ oz neat syrup	1 bar spoon neat syrup
$1/2$ oz neat syrup	2 bar spoons neat syrup

N.B. If you are using a household teaspoon instead of a bar spoon, remember that a bar spoon is a little smaller than a teaspoon.

THE WEAK: ICE

Different glasses suit different sizes & shapes of ice. A coupe glass suits small balls, highball glasses suit large cubes while a rocks glass looks marvellous with a single large sphere of ice.

Large ice cubes melt more slowly &, given a watery drink is no fun at all, go mostly for large spheres or cubes when you buy your ice trays. Avoid cracked ice - it melts too quickly to be of use - & avoid shaved ice because it's a headache to make & rewards you with a sudden head cold when you drink it.

WHAT YOU'LL NEED: INGREDIENTS

THE STRONG: WINE, LIQUORS & LIQUEURS

Don't try to keep everything in stock. Refer to the following pages to help you decide what suits you & your friends. I always keep gin, vodka, gold rum, tequila & Cointreau at home, but if you want to start lightly, just a gold rum & a tequila will give you plenty of cocktail options.

WINES & FORTIFIED WINES

Champagne (only use Prosecco if you have to).
Dry white vermouth

LIQUORS

Liquors (distilled spirits) form the base of most mixed drinks:

Brandy (distilled from fruit, generally grapes).
Gin (distilled from grain and juniper berries).
Cachaça (distilled from cane juice, essential only in a Caipirinha).
Pisco (distilled from fermented grape juice, essential only in a Pisco Sour).
Rum (see p19).
Tequila (distilled from blue agave, or mezcal distilled from any agave. Tequila reposado is aged for a year in oak barrels).
Vodka (distilled from potatoes).
Whiskey & Bourbon (distilled from fermented grain).

LIQUEURS

A liqueur is a distilled spirit to which a sweetener & flavour has been added.
Liqueurs often act as a substitute for the 'sweet' or syrup element
in cocktails:

Almond Liqueur (a base spirit flavoured with almond pits).
Coffee Liqueur (a base spirit blended with caffeine).
Whiskey Cream Liqueur (an emulsion of cream & whiskey).
Triple Sec (a base spirit flavoured with orange).

A NOTE ON COFFEE LIQUEURS

Most are filthy. Mr Black's is excellent & FAIR Cafe Liqueur is good.
Unless you're flat broke, avoid everything else.

A NOTE ON WHISKEY CREAM LIQUEURS

Kyrö ideally, Baileys only if you have to.

A NOTE ON TRIPLE SEC

Orange liqueurs are variable & very confusing. Go for Triple Sec by FAIR
or Cointreau or Clément Creole Shrubb. Avoid Grand Marnier - it's tricky
as a mixer. The rest are all either artificially sweet & sticky & should at all
costs be avoided.

AN INTRODUCTION TO RUMS

With just an honest rum, fresh citrus & cold ice you'll make some of the finest cocktails there are. Keep a gold rum in stock - it covers most bases - but you'll need the Brazilian rum, cachaça, in a Caipirinha.

There are no rules governing the production of most rums. Many different raw materials are used (sugar cane juice, sugar cane syrup, molasses etc) making rum one of the most diverse & confusing categories of alcohol on the planet, so here's an absolute beginner's guide:

MOLASSES RUMS

GOLD OR AMBER RUMS: fairly loose terms but the longer a rum is matured, the darker it becomes. Nevertheless, beware - darker doesn't always mean better - it could be that a particular kind of barrel has been used to mature it or that colourings have been added.

SPANISH OR SOLERA RUMS: a continuous ageing process, with the new spirit starting at the top row of casks & slowly moving down until the rum is extracted for bottling.

BLACK, BLACKSTRAP OR MOLASSES RUMS: robust rums, supposedly made from molasses or the last processing of sugar cane but often colouring has been added.

DEMERARA: gold & light amber in colour, distilled in Guyana, aged in wood casks for a year or so.

LIGHT, WHITE OR SILVER RUMS: another loose term. These can be clear, light rums or they can be clear, pure, pot still rums with a full intense flavour.

SPICED RUMS: possibly aged, generally combined with artificial flavourings. I don't know anyone over 25 who would drink them.

SUGAR CANE JUICE RUMS

CACHAÇA: produced in Brazil under strict national rules. Made from sugar cane juice & very good indeed.

RHUM AGRICOLE: produced in the French Caribbean, under strict national rules, from sugar cane juice. Has a fresh, grassy flavour. Can be very good, especially in Daiquiris or Mojitos.

WHAT YOU'LL NEED: INGREDIENTS

MIXERS

Pink lemonade (for The Girlfriend only).
Mexican cola (which, unlike Coca Cola, has no artificial sweeteners.
For the Cuba Libre only).
Soda water (Schweppes has the best carbonation or use a Soda Stream).

BITTERS

Bitters make all the difference: consider them a tonic or medicinal & feel
virtuous as you add them. They're a fun, easy way to add flavour so use
them the way you'd use garlic or chilli in your cooking. If you only want
to buy one kind of bitter then go for aromatic. I keep three in stock;
aromatic, orange & chilli.

Aromatic: great with rums, champagne cocktails & fizzes. Angostura,
Fee Brothers, The Bitter Truth, Peychauds & Old Time are good brands.
Orange: bright & zesty, good in Margaritas, Martinis & Daiquiris.
Grapefruit: great with Daiquiris & all summery rum cocktails.
Chilli: Bittermens Hellfire is wonderful for a fiery kick.

FRUIT & HERBS

You won't need all of these but there is no way around the fresh limes
& lemons.

Banana (Samantha, West Coast Cooler).
Cucumber (Spring Clean, Slim & Soda, Cloverita).
Grapefruit juice, pink if you can get it (Paloma only).
Jalapeño pepper (Maria Sangrienta & Spicy Margarita only).
Lemons (must be fresh).
Lime (must be fresh).
Mango (West Coast Cooler only).
Mint (essential in a Mojito & Mint Julep only).
Orange (Debutante, Duchess & Old Fashioned only).

Passionfruit juice, unsweetened (Perfect Lady, Debutante).

Pineapple fruit/juice, unsweetened (Piña Colada, West Coast Cooler, Painkiller).

Watermelon fruit/juice, unsweetened (Painkiller, Pink Margarita, Toy Boy, Watermelon Hi & West Coast Cooler).

PANTRY STAPLES

You won't need all of these by any means & you're likely to have many of them anyway.

Coconut cream unsweetened (I use Biona, any other works too, but avoid Cream of Coconut, it has a very syrupy consistency).

Condensed coconut cream (for an Island Dream only, I use Biona).

Coffee

Eggs (always optional & for creating froth only).

Nutmeg

Pepper

Syrup of choice (I use light agave, yacon or coconut blossom).

Demerara sugar (Mojito & Caipirinha only).

Sea salt (flaky)

Whipping cream (I love the Coconut Collaborative vegan double cream but dairy cream works just as well).

PANTRY STAPLES FOR A MARIA SANGRIENTA ONLY:

Tomato juice

Celery salt or Tajin

Green olive

Tabasco or other hot sauce

All spirits, syrups, bitters & mixers are easily available at www.amathusdrinks.com

WHAT YOU CAN MAKE WITH WHAT YOU'VE GOT

(bracketed items are ideal but not essential)

IF YOU HAVE AMARETTO
Amaretto Sour (p85) Amaretto, lemons, aromatic bitters

IF YOU HAVE BOURBON
Mint Julep (p65) bourbon, syrup, mint
Old Fashioned (p101) bourbon, syrup, (aromatic or orange bitters)

IF YOU HAVE CACHAÇA
Caipirinha (p70) cachaça, limes, sugar

IF YOU HAVE CHAMPAGNE (& TRIPLE SEC)
Debutante (p32) champagne, triple sec, passionfruit juice, orange bitters, (orange twist)
Duchess (p32) champagne, orange & grapefruit bitters, (orange twist)

IF YOU HAVE COFFEE LIQUEUR
Espresso Martini (p93) vodka, coffee liqueur, coffee

IF YOU HAVE GIN (& TRIPLE SEC & AMARETTO)
Perfect Lady (p36) gin, passionfruit juice, lemons, syrup (egg white)
White Lady (p77) gin, triple sec, lemons, agave (Amaretto, egg white)

IF YOU HAVE PISCO
Pisco Sour (p86) pisco, lemons, limes, syrup (egg white, aromatic bitters)

IF YOU HAVE RUM
Bajan Rum Punch (p27) rum, limes, syrup (nutmeg, aromatic or orange bitters)
Cuba Libre (p81) rum, cola, limes
Calypso Coffee (p94) rum, (coconut) whipping cream, coffee, sugar, nutmeg
Daiquiri (p69) rum, limes, syrup (orange or grapefruit bitters)
Island Dream (p49) rum, coconut cream, condensed coconut milk
Mojito (p53) rum, limes, syrup, mint (soda)

Painkiller (p107) rum, pineapple, coconut cream, passionfruit juice

Piña Colada (p46) rum, pineapple, coconut cream, limes, syrup

Rum Sour (p89) rum, lemons, syrup (egg white, aromatic bitters)

Samantha (p108) rum, banana, coconut cream, syrup (mint)

West Coast Cooler (p50) rum, banana, watermelon, mango, pineapple, syrup

IF YOU HAVE **RUM & TRIPLE SEC**

Cobblers Sidecar (p73) rum, triple sec, lemons (aromatic bitters)

IF YOU HAVE **TEQUILA**

Cloverita (p43) tequila, cucumber, lime, syrup

Maria Sangrienta (p104) tequila, tomato juice, jalapeño pepper, lemons, chilli bitters, celery salt or Tajin, hot sauce, pepper

Paloma (p54) tequila, grapefruit, limes, syrup (salt, soda)

Spicy Margarita (p97) tequila, limes, syrup, jalapeño pepper

Tequila Fizz (p30) tequila, limes, syrup, egg white (aromatic bitters, soda, mint)

Toy Boy (p40) tequila, limes, watermelon juice, syrup

IF YOU HAVE **TEQUILA & TRIPLE SEC**

Coconut Margarita (p57) tequila, triple sec, coconut cream, limes

Margarita (p61) tequila, triple sec, limes, syrup, salt

Pink Margarita (p62) tequila, triple sec, watermelon, syrup

Girlfriend (p66) tequila, triple sec, lemons, lemonade or soda

IF YOU HAVE **VODKA**

Slim & Soda (p35) vodka, limes, mint, syrup, soda (cucumber)

Spring Clean (p39) vodka, lemons, cucumber, syrup (mint, soda)

Watermelon Hi (p29) vodka, watermelon, limes, soda

IF YOU HAVE **VODKA & VERMOUTH**

Vesper (p98) vodka, vermouth, gin (grapefruit or orange bitters)

Vodka Martini (p74) vodka, vermouth (lemon twist or chilli bitters)

IF YOU HAVE **WHISKEY CREAM LIQUEUR & RUM OR VODKA**

Flat White Martini (p90) vodka, whiskey cream liqueur, coffee

Kickstart (p82) rum, whiskey cream liqueur, nutmeg

BRUNCH & LUNCH

BAJAN RUM PUNCH

Chilled rocks glass filled with large ice cubes
(to serve)

2 oz gold rum
2 oz lime juice (juice of 2 limes)
1 bar spoon or $^1/_4$ oz neat syrup
2 dashes of aromatic bitters
Wedge of lime (to dress)
Fresh nutmeg (to dress)

Add rum, lemon & syrup to the rocks glass full of
ice. Stir. Dot with bitters of choice.
Dress with a wedge of lime wheel & sprinkle with
freshly grated nutmeg.

SOME OF SOUR, LESS OF SWEET,
SOME OF STRONG, MORE OF WEAK,
A DASH OF BITTERS & A SPRINKLE OF SPICE,
SERVE WELL CHILLED WITH PLENTY OF ICE.

WATERMELON HI

Chilled highball glass filled with small ice cubes (to serve)

2 oz vodka
3 oz watermelon juice, strained
1 oz lime juice (juice of 1 lime)
Soda to top up
Straw (to dress)
Lime wheel (to dress)

Add all ingredients to the highball filled with ice.
Stir & top up with soda. Serve with a straw & a lime wheel.

LIGHT & EASY.

TEQUILA FIZZ

Chilled highball glass filled with small
ice cubes (to serve)

2 oz tequila
1 oz lime juice (juice of 1 lime)
A dash of neat syrup, optional
1 egg white
Soda to top up
Aromatic bitters (to serve)
Mint sprig (to serve)

Dry shake (no ice) all ingredients except the
soda. Pour into a highball glass full of ice. Top
up with soda. Add bitters & a sprig of mint if
wished.

CLEAN AS A WHISTLE.

THE DEBUTANTE

Chilled coupe glass (to serve)

1 oz passionfruit juice, unsweetened
(optional)
4 oz champagne, rosé is pretty
¹/₄ oz triple sec
A dash of orange bitters
A twist of any citrus (to dress)

Pour the juice & triple sec into a
coupe glass. Top up with chilled
champagne.
Add a dash of orange bitters
& dress with a twist of citrus.

THE DUCHESS

Chilled coupe glass (to serve)

5 oz chilled champagne, rosé is pretty
A dash of orange bitters
3 dashes of grapefruit bitters
A twist of any citrus (to dress)

Pour the champagne into a coupe glass, add the
bitters & dress with a twist of citrus.
Easy, chic, practically medicinal.

**BOTH COCKTAILS COULD ALSO BE
SERVED IN A ROCKS GLASS OVER A
LARGE BLOCK OR BALL OF ICE.**

THE SLIM & SODA

Chilled highball glass filled with large ice cubes
(to serve)

2 oz vodka
$^1/_2$ oz fresh lime juice (juice of $^1/_2$ lime)
10 mint leaves
A dash of neat syrup, only if you need it
2 inches cucumber (optional)
Soda to top up
Mint sprig (to dress)
Lime wedge (to dress)
Curl of cucumber (optional, to dress)
Straw (to dress)

Muddle the mint & cucumber (if using) in a shaker.
Add the vodka, lime juice & if needed, the syrup. Shake.
Pour over the highball full of ice. Top up with soda to
taste. Dress with a sprig of mint, a curl of cucumber, a
wedge of lime & a straw.

SLIM AS A RAKE.

PERFECT LADY

Chilled coupe glass (to serve)
A rocks glass worth of small ice cubes (to shake)

2 oz gin
$^1/_2$ oz lemon juice (juice of $^1/_2$ lemon)
1 oz passionfruit juice
1 bar spoon or $^1/_4$ oz neat syrup
1 egg white (optional)
Twist of lemon (to dress)

Shake all the ingredients (except the ice) in the shaker
to create a foam. Add the ice, shake again, then pour
into the chilled coupe glass & dress with a twist of
lemon.

SMART & BOLD.

THE SPRING CLEAN

Chilled highball glass filled with large ice cubes
(to serve)

3 inches cucumber
2 oz of vodka
1 oz fresh lemon juice (juice of 1 lemon)
1 bar spoon or $^1/_4$ oz neat syrup (optional)
Sprig of mint (to dress)
Straw (to dress)

Blend the cucumber & syrup. Strain into a shaker. Add
the lemon juice & vodka. Shake. Strain into a highball
filled with ice & fresh mint leaves.
Add a dash of soda if you'd like. Dress with a sprig of mint
& a straw.

CONSIDER THIS A TONIC.

THE TOY BOY

Chilled coupe, Martini or Margarita glass (to serve)
A rocks glass worth of large ice cubes (to shake)

Lime & sea salt to rim the glass (optional)
2 $^1/_2$ oz tequila
1 oz lime juice (juice of 1 lime)
A dash of neat syrup
3 oz watermelon juice (use a blender on a chunk of cold watermelon)
Twist of lime (to serve)

Rim the coupe glass with lime & salt if you like (I don't).
Add all ingredients including ice to a shaker & shake.
Pour into the chilled coupe glass & dress with a
twist of lime.

THE PERFECT ACCESSORY.

CLOVERITA

Chilled Margarita or Martini glass (to serve)
A rocks glass worth of small ice cubes (to shake)

2 oz tequila reposado
3 inches of cucumber
1 oz or less fresh lime juice (juice of 1 lime)
1 bar spoon or $^1/_4$ oz neat syrup
Twist of lime (to dress)
A curl of cucumber (to dress)

Blend or muddle the cucumber well, then add all the ingredients including ice, to a shaker & shake hard. Strain into the chilled glass, dress with a twist of lime & a strip of cucumber.

HEAVEN.

PIÑA COLADA

Chilled hurricane or highball glass (to serve)
A hurricane glass worth of small ice cubes
(to shake)

2 oz gold rum
4 oz fresh pineapple juice or chunks
2 oz coconut cream, unsweetened
$^1/_2$ oz fresh lime juice (juice of $^1/_2$ lime)
1 bar spoon or $^1/_4$ oz neat syrup
Straw (to dress)

Combine all the ingredients, including
the ice, in a blender & blend. Tip into a
hurricane glass if you have one, or a highball
if you don't.
People dress this cocktail with all manner of
things but a pretty straw is all you need.

DON'T PRETEND YOU DON'T LIKE IT.

ISLAND DREAM

Chilled rocks glass filled with ice cubes (to serve)
A rocks glass worth of small ice cubes (to shake)

2 oz gold rum or cachaça
2 oz coconut cream
1 oz condensed coconut milk
Straw (to dress)

Add the coconut milk, coconut cream, ice & gold rum or cachaça to a shaker. Shake until frothy, pour, top up with more ice cubes & serve with a straw, if preferred.

FINANCE BRO FANTASY.

WEST COAST COOLER

Chilled hurricane glass filled with small ice cubes
(to serve)

4 oz gold rum
6 oz watermelon chunks
4 oz or $^1/_4$ of a banana
4 oz or $^1/_4$ of a mango
4 oz pineapple juice (unsweetened)
or fresh pineapple chunks
A dash of neat syrup
Straw (to dress)

Blend all the ingredients including ice, then pour into
the chilled glass. Dress with a stripy straw (& a hibiscus
flower if you have one to hand).

THE TROPICS IN A GLASS, THIS IS BEST
DRUNK ON THE WEST COAST OF BARBADOS
AT COBBLERS COVE.

MOJITO

Chilled highball glass filled with small ice cubes (to serve)

2 oz white rum (ridiculously good with a Rhum Agricole)
1 lime
12 mint leaves
1 tbsp demerara sugar (or $^1/_2$ oz neat syrup)
Soda to top up
A sprig of mint (to dress)
Straw (to dress)

Quarter the limes into the glass, add the sugar & mint & muddle well. Add the rum & stir. Fill the glass with small ice cubes, top up with soda & stir well. Add mint & a straw to dress.

TO MAKE A MOSQUITO, SUBSTITUTE THE RUM WITH PISCO.

IF YOU MUST HAVE IT VIRGIN, REPLACE THE RUM WITH AN EQUAL QUANTITY OF LIME & SODA.

PALOMA

Chilled highball glass filled with large ice cubes
(to serve)

Sea salt (to rim the glass)
1 $^3/_4$ oz tequila
1 $^3/_4$ oz grapefruit juice, pink if possible
$^3/_4$ oz fresh lime juice (juice of $^3/_4$ lime)
1 bar spoon or $^1/_4$ oz neat syrup
Soda to top up
Twist or a wheel of lime (to dress)

Rim the glass with lime juice & salt & set aside. Shake the
tequila, syrup, grapefruit & lime juices together, strain or
just dump into a chilled highball full of ice. Top up with
soda & dress with a wheel or twist of lime. No straw.

ANYTIME,
ANY PLACE,
ANYWHERE.

COCONUT MARGARITA

Chilled Margarita glass (to serve)
A rocks glass worth of small ice cubes (to shake)

1^1/$_2$ oz tequila reposado
1 oz triple sec
2 oz coconut cream, unsweetened
^{1}/$_2$ oz lime juice, to taste (juice of ^{1}/$_2$ lime)
Twist of lime (to dress)

Add all ingredients including the ice to a shaker. Shake well, strain into the Margarita glass & dress with a twist of lime & ice if you like.

JUST FLOAT THROUGH THE AFTERNOON ON ONE OF THESE.....

'I LIKE TO HAVE A MARTINI,
TWO AT THE VERY MOST -
AFTER THREE I'M UNDER THE TABLE,
AFTER FOUR I'M UNDER MY HOST.'
- DOROTHY PARKER

THE COCKTAIL HOUR

MARGARITA

Chilled rocks or Margarita glass filled with ice cubes (to serve)
A rocks glass worth of large ice cubes (to shake)

Lime juice & sea salt (to rim the glass, optional)
2 oz tequila reposado
$^1/_2$ oz triple sec
1 oz lime juice (or the juice of 1 lime)
1 bar spoon or $^1/_4$ oz neat syrup, to taste
1 lime wheel (to dress)

Rim the rocks or Margarita glass with salt if you like (I don't) & set aside.
Add a rocks glass worth of ice & all other ingredients to a shaker. Then shake until well chilled. Strain into the chilled rocks or Margarita glass, add more ice cubes if desired. Dress with a lime wheel.

Make it a Mexican Martini by serving straight up in a coupe glass with a pimiento-stuffed green olive & a splash of olive juice.

Make it a Mezcalita by using mezcal.

ONE TEQUILA,
TWO TEQUILA,
THREE TEQUILA,
FLOOR.

PINK MARGARITA

Chilled Margarita or coupe glass (to serve)
A rocks glass worth of small ice cubes (to shake)

Lime juice & sea salt (to rim the glass, optional)
2 oz fresh watermelon juice (use a blender on a chunk of cold watermelon)
1 $1/2$ oz tequila
$1/4$ oz triple sec
$1/2$ oz lime juice (or the juice of $1/2$ a lime)
 A dash of neat syrup, optional, to taste
Twist of lime (to dress)

Rim a Margarita glass with lime & salt if you like (I don't) & set aside.
Blend the watermelon. Add the watermelon, ice, tequila, triple sec & lime to a shaker. Shake. Strain into the chilled Margarita glass & serve straight up with a twist of lime.

Or serve in a rocks glass over ice, as you prefer.

LA VIE EN ROSE.

MINT JULEP

Chilled rocks glass filled with small cubes of ice (to serve)

2 oz bourbon
10 mint leaves
1 bar spoon or ¼ oz neat syrup
Sprig of mint (to dress)
Straw (to dress)

Muddle the mint leaves with the syrup in the glass, add the bourbon, pack the glass with ice & stir well. Dress with a sprig of mint & a straw.

YOU CAN'T GO WRONG.
A SOPHISTICATED CLASSIC.

THE GIRLFRIEND

Chilled rocks glass filled with large ice cubes (to serve)

Salt
2 oz tequila
1 oz triple sec
3 oz pink lemonade (or soda)
$^1/_2$ oz lemon juice (juice of $^1/_2$ lemon)
Twist of lemon (to dress)

Rim the glass with salt, fill with ice & set aside.
Stir the pink lemonade, lemon juice, triple sec & tequila
together in a shaker. Pour into the ice-filled glass. Dress
with a twist of lemon.

A friend of the Margarita.

YOU NEED A GIRLFRIEND TO PUT
THE WORLD TO RIGHTS.

DAIQUIRI

Chilled coupe or Margarita glass filled with small ice cubes (to serve)

2 oz gold rum (or rhum agricole)
2 bar spoons or $^1/_2$ oz neat syrup
1 $^1/_4$ oz lime juice (juice of 1 $^1/_4$ limes)
A dash of orange or grapefruit bitters
Twist or wheel of lime (to dress)

Shake all ingredients, including ice, in a shaker, strain into your chilled glass. Add the bitters & dress with a twist of lime. Top up with ice if you like.

Don't mess this drink about with bananas, strawberries etc - this classic lime Daiquiri is just so clean & smart.

HEMINGWAY TOOK HIS
WITHOUT SUGAR.

CAIPIRINHA

Chilled rocks glass filled with ice cubes (to serve)
A rocks glass worth of small ice cubes (to shake)

2 oz cachaça
2 limes, quartered
2 tsps or less of caster, demerara or muscovado sugar
Straw (to dress)

Quarter the limes into the glass, add the sugar & muddle
well. Fill the glass with ice, add the cachaça & stir.

Cachaça is made straight from fresh sugarcane,
unlike rum which is made from the by-products
of sugar production.

BOTTLED SUNSHINE.

COBBLERS SIDECAR

Chilled coupe glass filled with small ice cubes (to serve)
A rocks glass worth of small cubes (to shake)

1 ¹/₂ oz gold rum
¹/₂ oz lemon juice (juice of ¹/₂ lemon)
¹/₂ oz triple sec
A dash of aromatic bitters
Twist of lemon (to dress)

Add everything except the bitters to a shaker & shake.
Pour into the glass.
Express a twist of lemon over the drink, rub it around the rim of the glass & drop it in.
Add a dash of bitters.

To make a classic Sidecar, replace the rum with cognac.

KEEP YOUR OPTIONS OPEN.

VODKA MARTINI

Chilled Martini or coupe glass (to serve)
A rocks glass worth of large ice cubes (to shake)

2 $^1/_2$ oz vodka
$^1/_4$ oz white vermouth
Twist of lemon (to serve)

Add the ice, vodka & vermouth to a shaker or jug. Shake, then strain into the chilled glass. Express the lemon twist over the liquid, then drop the peel into the glass.

For a twist on this classic Vodka Martini, add a dash of chilli bitters.

Make it a Dirty Martini with a green olive or Extra Dirty with an olive & juice from the olive jar.

Make it a Gin Martini by replacing the vodka with a dry gin.

SO ELEGANT & SO EFFECTIVE.

WHITE LADY

Chilled rocks glass filled with large ice cubes (to serve)

2 oz gin
1 oz triple sec
2 oz lemon juice (juice of 2 lemons)
1 egg white (I prefer without)
A dash of Amaretto
Twist of lemon (to dress)

Add all ingredients except ice to a shaker & dry shake.
Pour into the rocks glass over the large ice cubes.
Express the lemon twist over the drink & drop the peel
into the glass.

A SHOWSTOPPER.

INTO THE NIGHT

CUBA LIBRE

Chilled highball glass filled with large ice cubes (to serve)

2 oz rum, any will do, except spiced
$3/4$ oz lime juice (juice of $3/4$ a lime)
4 oz cola (ideally Mexican)
2 lime wedges at least (to dress)

Pour the rum over the ice in the chilled highball glass & stir briefly.
Add the lime juice & cola, stir once. Dunk in the lime wedges & stir again.

KEEP THE PARTY GOING.

THE KICKSTART

Chilled coupe glass (to serve)
A coupe glass worth of small ice cubes (to shake)

2 oz rum
1.75 oz whiskey cream liqueur
Nutmeg, optional (to dress)

Shake the rum, whiskey cream liqueur & the ice in a
shaker. Strain into the coupe glass.
Grate a generous sprinkling of nutmeg over it.

ROCKET FUEL.

AMARETTO SOUR

Chilled rocks glass ideally with one large sphere
or several large cubes of ice (to serve)
A rocks glass worth of large ice cubes (to shake)

2 oz Amaretto
Juice of 1 lemon
Drop of aromatic bitters (optional)
Twist of lime, lemon or orange (to dress)

Shake the ice cubes, lemon juice & Amaretto together
in a shaker. Strain into a rocks glass over the ice.
Add a drop of bitters (if using) but don't stir.
Dress with a twist of citrus, any citrus will do.

THE PERFECT
AFTER DINNER COCKTAIL.

PISCO SOUR

Chilled coupe or Martini glass (to serve)
A rocks glass worth of small cubes ice cubes (to shake)

2 oz pisco
Juice of $^1/_2$ lemon
Juice of $^1/_2$ lime
2 bar spoons or $^1/_2$ oz neat syrup
Egg white (optional)
A dash of aromatic bitters (optional)
Twist of lime (to dress)

If you are using egg white, dry shake all the ingredients.
Then shake all ingredients with the ice. If not using egg
white (I don't) simply shake all ingredients with the ice.
Strain into the chilled coupe. Dot the top of the foam
with the bitters (if using) & dress with a twist of lime.

KNOCKOUT.

RUM, WHISKEY OR BOURBON SOUR

Chilled rocks glass filled with ice cubes (to serve)
A rocks glass worth of small ice cubes (to shake)

2 oz gold rum, bourbon or whiskey
Juice of 1 lemon
2 bar spoons or $^1/_2$ oz neat syrup
Egg white, optional
A dash of aromatic bitters (optional)
Lemon wheel (to dress)

Add the strong, the sour, the sweet & the egg white (if using) to a shaker & give a good strong shake to froth it up. Add the ice & shake again. Strain into the chilled glass. Dot the foam with bitters (if using) & dress with a lemon wheel.

ONE OF THESE & THE
WORLD IS YOURS...

FLAT WHITE MARTINI

Chilled Martini or coupe glass (to serve)
A rocks glass full of small ice cubes
(to shake)

3 oz whiskey cream liqueur
2 oz freshly brewed espresso coffee
Coffee beans (to dress)
1 oz vodka (optional)

Add all ingredients to a very clean shaker.
Shake until blended & silky. Strain into
the chilled glass & dress with coffee beans
if you like.

JUST PERFECT, SMOOTH & EASY.

ESPRESSO MARTINI

Chilled Martini glass (to serve)
A rocks glass full of small ice cubes (to shake)

1 oz vodka
1 oz coffee liqueur
2 oz freshly brewed espresso coffee
Coffee beans, optional (to dress)

Shake all ingredients & ice in a cocktail shaker & strain
into the chilled Martini glass.
If you have any to hand, add coffee beans to the surface
to dress it up.

If you don't take sugar in your coffee then don't take it in
your Espresso Martini either.

THE BEST PICK-ME-UP,
WORKS AROUND THE CLOCK.

CALYPSO COFFEE

Mug or latte glass warmed (to serve)
A refrigerated bowl (for whipping the cream)

1-2 oz gold rum
4 oz approx.fresh whipping cream (dairy or unsweetened coconut)
3 oz strong, hot, freshly brewed cafetière coffee
A dash of neat syrup,optional (Coconut Blossom syrup works well here)
Freshly grated nutmeg (to dress)

Whip the cream & syrup together until it forms soft peaks. Add the rum
& hot coffee to the warmed glass & stir. Spoon the cream on top (aim at
$^1/_4$ cream to $^3/_4$ coffee mix).
When the heat of the coffee melts the cream into a foamy, floating layer,
sprinkle with freshly grated nutmeg.

F.D.A. APPROVED BUT THIS WILL KEEP YOU
DANCING TILL THE SUN RISES.

SPICY MARGARITA

Chilled Margarita glass (to serve)
A rocks glass full of small ice cubes (to shake)

Lime & sea salt (to rim the glass, optional)
2 oz tequila reposado
Juice of 1 lime
2 bar spoons or $^1/_2$ oz neat syrup
4 slices of fresh jalapeño pepper
Twist of lime (to dress)

Rim the glass with lime & salt if you like (I don't) & set aside. Add tequila, lime juice, two slices of jalapeño pepper, syrup & ice to a shaker. Shake. Strain into the chilled glass. Dress with a twist of lime & the remaining slices of jalapeño.

KICKS LIKE A MULE.

VESPER

Chilled Martini glass filled with small ice cubes (to serve)
Martini glass filled with small ice cubes (to shake)

3 oz gin
1 oz vodka
10 ml white vermouth
2 dashes of grapefruit or orange bitters
Twist of lime or lemon (to dress)

Shake everything together with the ice, strain into the chilled glass over ice & dress with a twist of lime.

IN A LETTER ABOUT THE COCKTAIL HE INVENTED FOR BOND, FLEMING WROTE THAT HE HAD SAMPLED IT & FOUND IT 'UNPALATABLE.' THIS IS A BETTER RECIPE THAN FLEMING'S.

OLD FASHIONED

Chilled rocks glass filled with ice cubes (to serve)
A rocks glass worth of large cubes of ice (to shake)

2 oz bourbon
1-2 tsps demerara sugar (or maple syrup works well)
A dash of orange bitters
2 dashes of aromatic bitters
Wheel or twist of orange (to dress)

Mix the bitters & teaspoon of sugar in the chilled rocks
glass. Stir in the bourbon.
Tip into the rocks glass filled with ice.
Dress with an orange wheel or twist.

'THE ONLY COCKTAIL REALLY TO
RIVAL A MARTINI.' KINGSLEY AMIS

MARIA SANGRIENTA

Chilled highball or hurricane glass filled with large ice cubes (to serve)

2 oz tequila reposado
6 oz tomato juice
$^3/_4$ oz lime juice (juice of $^3/_4$ of a lime)
Jalapeño pepper, 3 slices
7 dashes of chilli bitters
6 dashes of Tabasco or other hot sauce
Celery salt or Tajin
Freshly ground pepper
Lime wheel (to dress)
Green olive (to dress)
Jalapeño pepper, 2 fine slices (to dress)
Straw (to dress)

TOTALLY MEDICINAL.

Muddle the 3 jalapeño slices in a shaker, add tomato & lime juice, tequila, pepper, celery salt or Tajin. Shake. Pour over the ice into the chilled glass.
Season with the bitters & hot sauce. Stir. Dress with a lime wheel, olive, two fine slices of jalapeño pepper & a straw.

To make this a plain, old Bloody Mary, replace the tequila with vodka, the lime with lemon & the jalapeño with a celery stick.

PAINKILLER

Chilled highball glass (to serve)
A highball glass full of small ice cubes
(to blend)

2 oz gold rum
2 oz pineapple chunks
1 oz coconut cream, unsweetened
1 oz of watermelon chunks
A dash of neat syrup (optional)
Grated nutmeg, optional (to dress)
Straw (to dress)

Add the ice & all ingredients to a blender
& blend. Pour directly into the chilled
highball glass, add more ice if desired.
Sprinkle with freshly grated nutmeg & add
a straw.

DOES WHAT IT SAYS ON THE TIN.

THE SAMANTHA

Chilled highball glass (to serve)
A highball glass full of large ice cubes (to shake)

2 oz gold rum
1 banana
2 oz coconut cream, unsweetened
A dash of neat syrup
Sprig of mint (to dress)
Straw (to dress)

Blend the rum, banana, ice, coconut cream & syrup in a blender then pour into the chilled highball. Add more ice if desired. Dress with a sprig of mint & a straw.

LOOKS LIKE A SMOOTHIE –
NO ONE WILL EVER KNOW ...

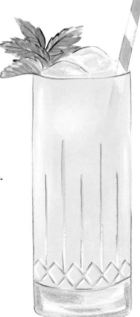

INDEX

WITH THANKS TO

Hugh, who makes the finest White Lady on the planet.

Stanley, my own in-house cocktelier, who has mixed every drink in this book many times over.

Lisa & Catharine, with whom I've drunk every cocktail in this book, many, many, many times over.

Isabelle, who has captured the spirit of every cocktail in this book.

Pearson, Virgil & all at Cobblers Cove, you are the best, no cocktail tastes as good anywhere else in the world.

Sam de Terán

November 2023